For Immediate Release
Contact: Maya Bradford
212.229.7188
mbradford@abramsbooks.com

ABRAMS The Art of Books
195 Broadway, New York, NY 10007
tel 212.206.7715 fax 212.519.1210
abramsbooks.com

One Year Wiser
An Illustrated Guide to Mindfulness

By Mike Medaglia

A new book to help young readers harness the power of meditation, gratitude, and loving kindness—and live healthier, happier lives

As we travel through the world, we are often faced with conflicts and challenges that cause unhappiness, fear, or anxiety. The practice of mindfulness has the power to transform this negativity into feelings of love, compassion, and positivity. In *One Year Wiser: An Illustrated Guide to Mindfulness* (SelfMadeHero; October 24th, 2017; $14.99; Paperback), illustrator and Zen Buddhism practitioner **Mike Medaglia** takes young readers on a journey of self-discovery. Exploring what mindfulness is and the benefits it can bring, readers will discover a simple yet powerful truth: peace, contentment, and happiness are inside us already, and all we need are the tools to access them.

Drawing on the four seasons and our deep connection to the natural world, this smart, accessible, and beautifully illustrated graphic novel is a great introduction for young readers to discover the art of living mindfully. Featuring lessons as simple as discovering the importance of smiling, Medaglia has created a truly user-friendly guide that makes learning about meditation and self-love easier than ever.

ONE YEAR WISER

AN ILLUSTRATED GUIDE TO MINDFULNESS

Mike Medaglia

First published 2017
by SelfMadeHero
139-141 Pancras Road
London NW1 1UN
www.selfmadehero.com

Written and illustrated by Mike Medaglia

Publishing Director: Emma Hayley
Sales & Marketing Manager: Sam Humphrey
Editorial & Production Manager: Guillaume Rater
UK Publicist: Paul Smith
US Publicist: Maya Bradford
Designer: Txabi Jones
With thanks to: Dan Lockwood

A CIP record for this book is available from the British Library

ISBN: 978-1-910593-38-7

10 9 8 7 6 5 4 3 2 1

Printed and bound in Slovenia

Dedicated to my father
FRANK MEDAGLIA

PART ONE

SPRING

Spring is about blossoming and letting yourself change and become. Taking steps with confidence towards a brighter future and a more sincere self.

In part one, we will explore the following topics:

Mindfulness
Love
Happiness
Meditation
Smiling
Valuing Oneself

MINDFULNESS is the practice of training our minds to stay focused and concentrated on the present moment.

And by staying focused on the present moment, we get to experience this life as we live it.

WE SPEND OUR LIVES IN STORIES

But, lost in stories, we end up missing the moments of our lives.

MINDFULNESS BRINGS US BACK.

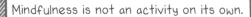

Mindfulness is not an activity on its own.

Instead, it is an active term that we can apply to whatever we are doing.

Mindful Walking

I am present as I walk along this path. The air is cool and I can hear birds singing in the trees.

Mindful Breathing

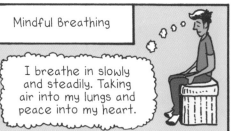

I breathe in slowly and steadily. Taking air into my lungs and peace into my heart.

I breathe out slowly and steadily. With my breath, I send out feelings of anxiety, fear and sadness.

Mindful Eating

Nom nom, this wrap is sooo good!

Practising mindfulness means coming back to the everlasting present. Being here and now. Grounded in peacefulness and experiencing our own nature.

The more we practise mindfulness, the more we can sustain our focus and so can draw upon it, not only at peaceful times but also when things get hectic and overwhelming.

When starting to practise mindfulness, do it in a quiet, comfortable and safe space.

Take time to sit and watch your breath in a place that makes you feel relaxed.

But as you practise more and more, you will find that you have mindful moments in places you would least expect them.

I am present.

I am present.

I am present.

LOSS

CONFRONTATION

AGGRESSION

Through mindfulness practice, when we face the moments of our lives that are challenging or upsetting, we will have the tools to draw upon and use.

SHAME

Not letting the uncomfortable or heartbreaking moments shatter our inner peace.

Throughout this book, we will talk about a number of different subjects.

Each chapter stands alone, but it should become clear that all these subjects are interconnected and create a web of support that you can lean on and use to help lift you up.

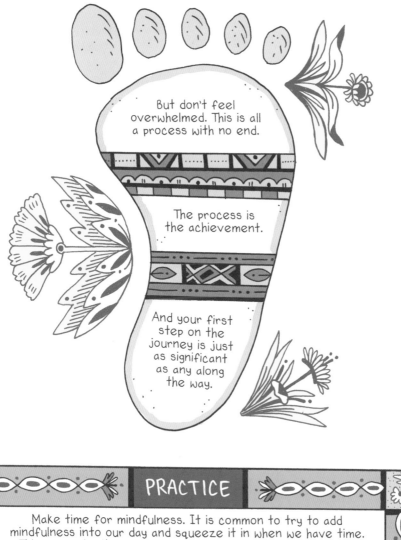

But don't feel overwhelmed. This is all a process with no end.

The process is the achievement.

And your first step on the journey is just as significant as any along the way.

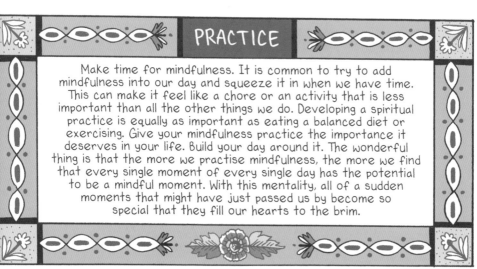

PRACTICE

Make time for mindfulness. It is common to try to add mindfulness into our day and squeeze it in when we have time. This can make it feel like a chore or an activity that is less important than all the other things we do. Developing a spiritual practice is equally as important as eating a balanced diet or exercising. Give your mindfulness practice the importance it deserves in your life. Build your day around it. The wonderful thing is that the more we practise mindfulness, the more we find that every single moment of every single day has the potential to be a mindful moment. With this mentality, all of a sudden moments that might have just passed us by become so special that they fill our hearts to the brim.

is
everything.

It really is.

Such an abstract concept. Super
hard to define in words. But the
fact of its existence is undeniable.

Love is safety.

Love is purpose.

Love is
learning who we are
as individuals through
the way we love others.

Love is
our greatest
antidote to hate.

Above all of this, love is much more than any possible effect it can have. To experience love is in itself the greatest experience we can have in this life.

Ground all your actions in a genuine, beneficial love, and love will sprout up around you like daffodils in the spring.

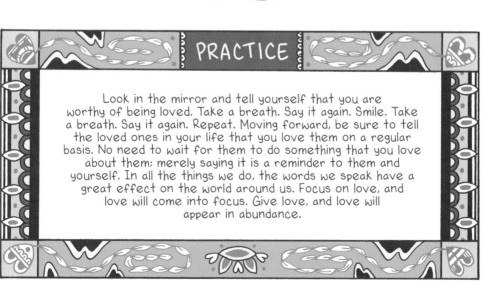

PRACTICE

Look in the mirror and tell yourself that you are worthy of being loved. Take a breath. Say it again. Smile. Take a breath. Say it again. Repeat. Moving forward, be sure to tell the loved ones in your life that you love them on a regular basis. No need to wait for them to do something that you love about them; merely saying it is a reminder to them and yourself. In all the things we do, the words we speak have a great effect on the world around us. Focus on love, and love will come into focus. Give love, and love will appear in abundance.

HAPPINESS

is different from indulgence.

It is not just about being happy with what you are doing at the moment.

Always moving from one activity to another in search of distraction.

Instead, happiness is the result of living well and living mindfully.

True happiness doesn't rely on any external factors.

The source of happiness is a well inside of us, and our actions fill that well with happiness we can draw upon.

This isn't to say that all moments will be happy.

But when we practise mindfulness, happiness always seems to be within our grasp.

And our lives become filled with so many more wonderful experiences.

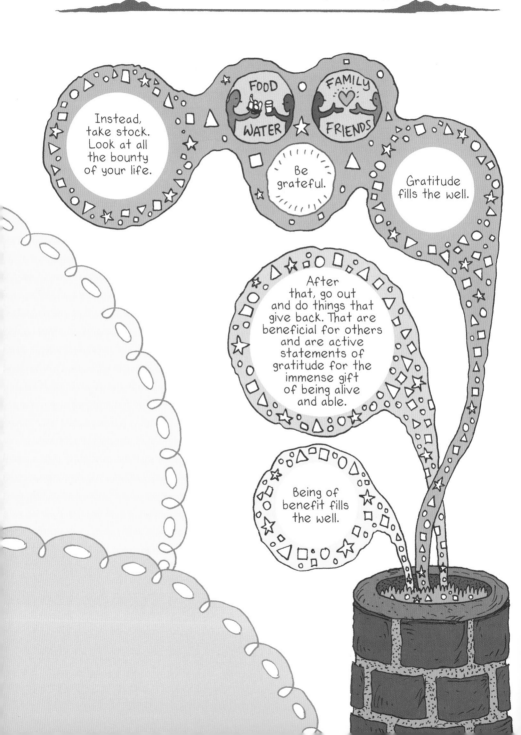

We do not achieve happiness.

Instead, we arrive at happiness as the result of mindful living, gratitude and beneficial activities.

PRACTICE

Make the little things in your day-to-day life big, important and wonderful. You may have had running clean water every day of your life, but it should still be a source of happiness every time you turn on the tap. You may walk the same street every time you go to work or school, but it should still be a place of awe and wonder as the birds fly around you, the sun shines and you are able to arrive at your destination safely. Happiness and contentment are already there, but they may be hiding in the seemingly mundane things around you. We are not owed anything in this life. Everything we have is a gift and a source of happiness that mindfulness practice can unlock. Mindfulness fills the well.

When we meditate, it is about becoming still.

A stillness in our bodies where we can focus on the natural process of our breathing.

Like a clock that we can only hear when the room goes silent.

Our breathing is very much like a clock. A reminder that life is moving. Not stagnant. And also not permanent.

Meditation is about giving our minds a chance to be still.
When we start to meditate, it is common to feel that as soon
as we sit down our thoughts jump all over the place.

Bouncing around every corner of our mind.

But the truth is that our minds are always like this, and only
when we become still and silent do we finally notice it.

So when we meditate, it is a constant process of bringing our minds back to focusing on the present moment.

And we can do this by focusing on our breathing.

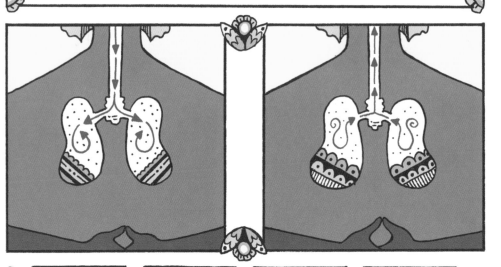

In and out.

In and out.

Here and now.

Here and now.

Inevitably your mind will wander. It is very natural. When this happens, just gently bring your mind back to your breathing.

Always with gentleness. Always with understanding.

This process is a chance to practise compassion towards oneself.

When we first start meditating on a regular basis, we will struggle. It is just a part of the process. At those times, one can use meditation as a way to check in with oneself.

Today I am anxious and a little sad.

Today I feel happy and that I made the most of the past twenty-four hours.

Today I am distracted and really just want to eat junk food and watch TV.

And there are so many ways to meditate. It is not all sitting on a cushion with crossed legs.

There is walking meditation.

We can pick a stretch of ground we walk down every day and say, "Whenever I walk this path, I am going to focus on my breathing and bring myself back to the present moment."

With meditation, there is actually nothing very special to achieve.

Some say that meditation is no big deal.

All we get is nothing.

But from that nothing, from that emptiness, we give ourselves the tools to be part of everything. To stop interfering with life and to let it unfold in the most natural of ways.

No big deal.

PRACTICE

It can be difficult to start meditating thirty to forty minutes a day and be super strict about it. Instead, start by meditating ten minutes a day for the first ten days. Then move on to twenty minutes for twenty days. Then thirty minutes for thirty days. If all goes to plan, you will then do forty minutes for forty years. But no pressure! A fun way to keep track of this is to collect ten pebbles. Lay them out in the area you like to meditate in and then after each session put one pebble into a little jar. This helps you keep track and is also a way to have the earth be a part of your practice. But don't be too strict. If you miss a few days, just keep going from where you left off.

SMILING

is an act of instant transformation.

I am constantly amazed by how effective it is.

I remember this one time I was travelling on a train. It had been a long day and I was heading home. It was a Friday, so the train was very busy and full of rowdy people enjoying themselves. I ended up standing crammed in a corner, surrounded by people who had the strong aroma of wine and beer.

THEN IT HAPPENED

I started smiling.

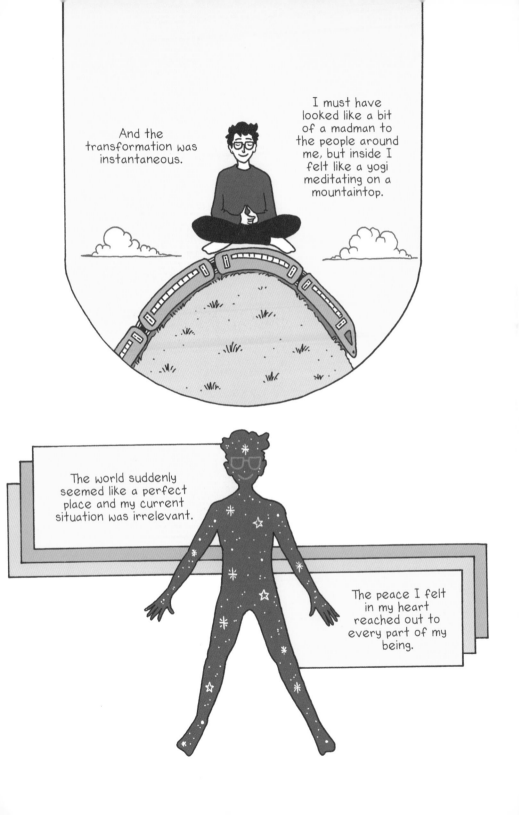

It is easy to
underestimate
or even forget

THE POWER OF SMILING

I am
smiling now

as I write this
in my local
coffee shop,
and it is having
the same
effect.

TAP
TAP
TAP

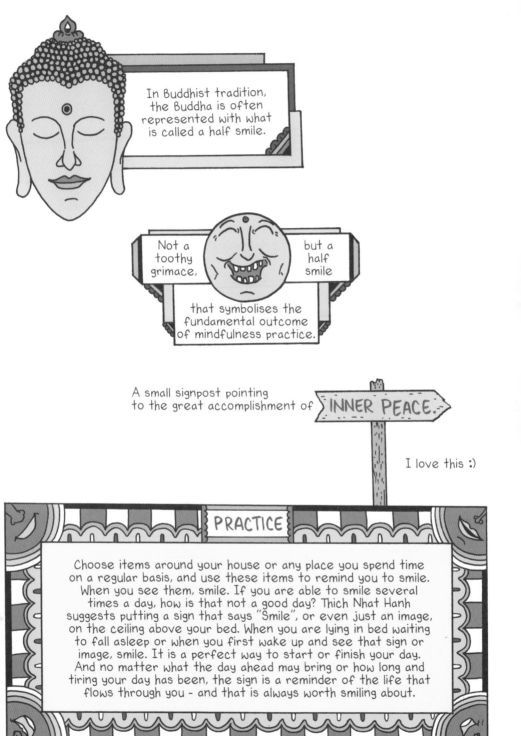

In Buddhist tradition, the Buddha is often represented with what is called a half smile.

Not a toothy grimace, but a half smile that symbolises the fundamental outcome of mindfulness practice.

A small signpost pointing to the great accomplishment of INNER PEACE.

I love this :)

PRACTICE

Choose items around your house or any place you spend time on a regular basis, and use these items to remind you to smile. When you see them, smile. If you are able to smile several times a day, how is that not a good day? Thich Nhat Hanh suggests putting a sign that says "Smile", or even just an image, on the ceiling above your bed. When you are lying in bed waiting to fall asleep or when you first wake up and see that sign or image, smile. It is a perfect way to start or finish your day. And no matter what the day ahead may bring or how long and tiring your day has been, the sign is a reminder of the life that flows through you - and that is always worth smiling about.

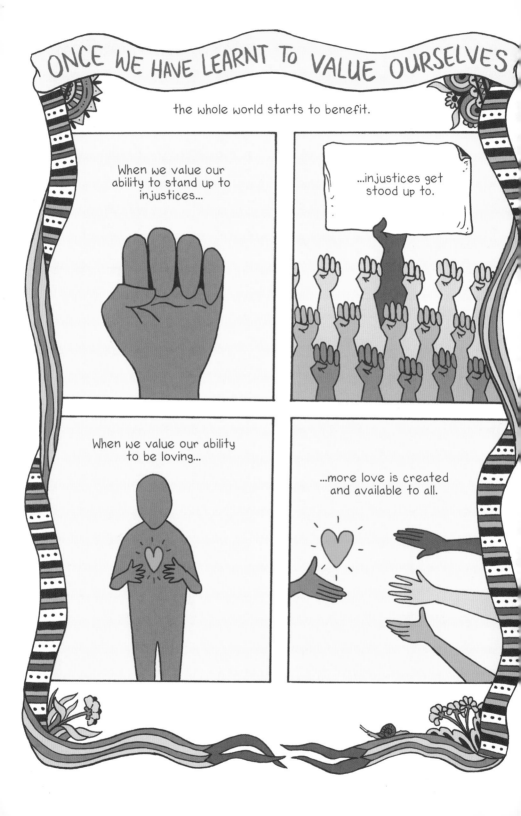

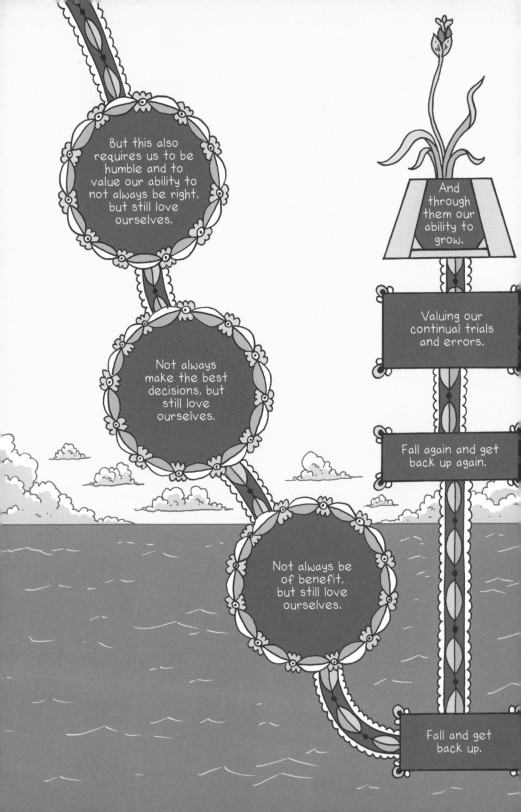

But this also requires us to be humble and to value our ability to not always be right, but still love ourselves.

Not always make the best decisions, but still love ourselves.

Not always be of benefit, but still love ourselves.

And through them our ability to grow.

Valuing our continual trials and errors.

Fall again and get back up again.

Fall and get back up.

Value yourself no matter what, and the world will benefit from your being.

Diminish yourself no matter what, and the world will lose out on so, so much.

I value you.

I hope you can see what I see.

PRACTICE

Make a habit of giving yourself positive reinforcement. On a daily basis, go over all of the good qualities that you admire in yourself. Even if this seems a bit silly or egotistical, it can really help to remind you how wonderful you are and all the things you have already achieved that are amazing. We can spend way too much time beating ourselves up or only focusing on what is wrong with us. Even your flaws can be a source of encouragement. If you are prone to being judgmental at times, think back. Maybe you were way more judgmental in your past than you are now. That is an encouraging sign that you are slowly leaving this trait behind. If you can learn to love yourself more, then you are creating more love in this world and that is such a wonderful thing.

PART TWO

SUMMER

In summer, we absorb, letting the light of love and happiness into our hearts, while using them to grow towards the sun.

In part two, we will explore the following topics:

Gratitude
Inner Growth
Friendship
Technology
Agitated Movement
Simplicity

gratitude

is a way of acknowledging the bounty of the present moment.

It is a simple practice, but one that can be applied to every single experience we have

I'm grateful for my time on this earth and the beauty I get to experience while here.

I'm grateful for the people in my life who treat me with kindness and help me believe in my potential.

I'm grateful for warm socks on cold days...

...and sandals in the summertime.

To be grateful for all the little things in our lives leads to overwhelming feelings of satisfaction and contentment.

And when we have come back to the present moment...

...it is much easier to appreciate all the wonderful (and often overlooked) things in our lives.

I call it looking at the world with grateful eyes.

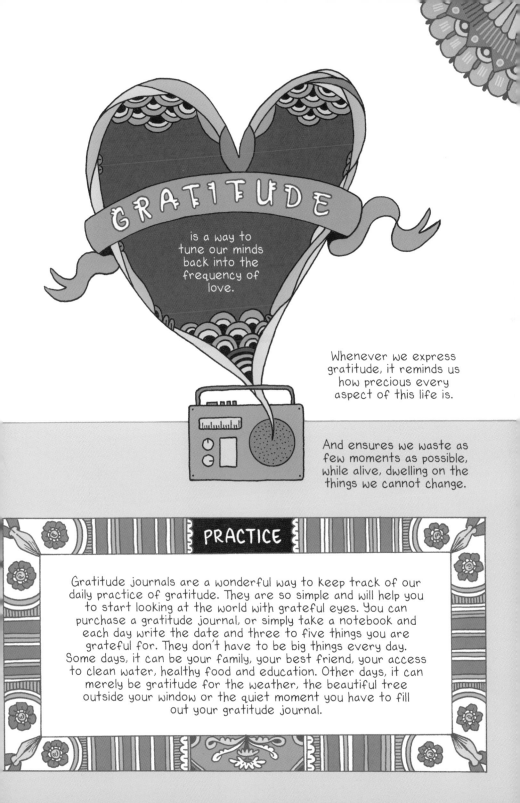

GRATITUDE

is a way to tune our minds back into the frequency of love.

Whenever we express gratitude, it reminds us how precious every aspect of this life is.

And ensures we waste as few moments as possible, while alive, dwelling on the things we cannot change.

PRACTICE

Gratitude journals are a wonderful way to keep track of our daily practice of gratitude. They are so simple and will help you to start looking at the world with grateful eyes. You can purchase a gratitude journal, or simply take a notebook and each day write the date and three to five things you are grateful for. They don't have to be big things every day. Some days, it can be your family, your best friend, your access to clean water, healthy food and education. Other days, it can merely be gratitude for the weather, the beautiful tree outside your window or the quiet moment you have to fill out your gratitude journal.

INNER GROWTH

 can often be ignored as we focus on the external things in our lives.

But without inner growth, we will always be chasing externals, looking to fill up the gaping empty holes within us.

DESIRES

THINGS

We think if we acquire more things or indulge our desires, then we will start to feel content.

INDULGENCES

EXTERNALS

STUFF

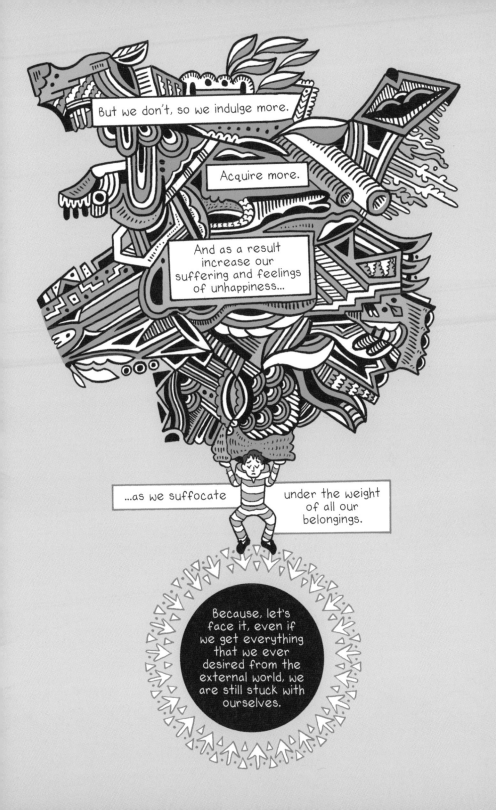

But when we take the time to meditate,

to practise mindfulness and increase our ability to focus on the present moment,

to contemplate our inner world

with compassion and understanding,

then we suddenly find that the external things we once desired seem less important.

Less necessary to being content.

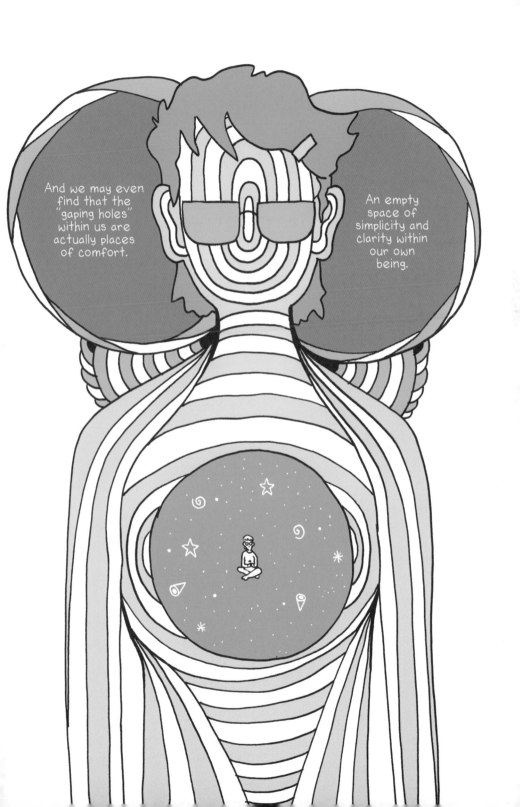

We can get lost and spend years wandering down paths of desire. Trying to accumulate
POWER, WEALTH
OR FAME
But there inevitably comes a day when we realise that it has all been in vain and all of these roads lead back to a single point.
The beginning of the path to ourselves.
Then, if we are lucky enough to have the courage,
we can start down the only path that actually leads to any form of growth and enduring happiness.
YOU COULD BE HERE

Instead, make the choice today. Choose the path of inner growth. Make a conscious decision to focus on your internal life. Then all the things you experience in your external life will benefit from the glow radiating inside you.

PRACTICE

Take time to sit with yourself. To quietly contemplate who you are on the inside. The thoughts you think. The mazes you are endlessly travelling through in your head. What is your motivation in life? What drives you forward? Do these things actually fulfill you or do they just give you a distraction or a vague hope of happiness that never seems to come to light? Are there ways you can simplify your pursuits and focus on things that give you peace? Love is the best way to grow internally. Are there ways to swap external pursuits with experiences of love for yourself and for all the people in your life? If so, focus on that. If not, try to give love and inner growth more importance in your everyday life.

But in revealing ourselves, we make ourselves vulnerable. We allow someone access to the part of ourselves that is the most susceptible to being bruised.

With the fewest of words.

Or the smallest of actions.

So there is certainly wisdom in choosing our friends with care and making sure they will take care with us.

If a friend causes you to feel upset, or to act in a way that is not in your best interest, then discuss these things with your friend.

If they keep occurring, take some time to think deeply about whether that is a friend worth keeping.

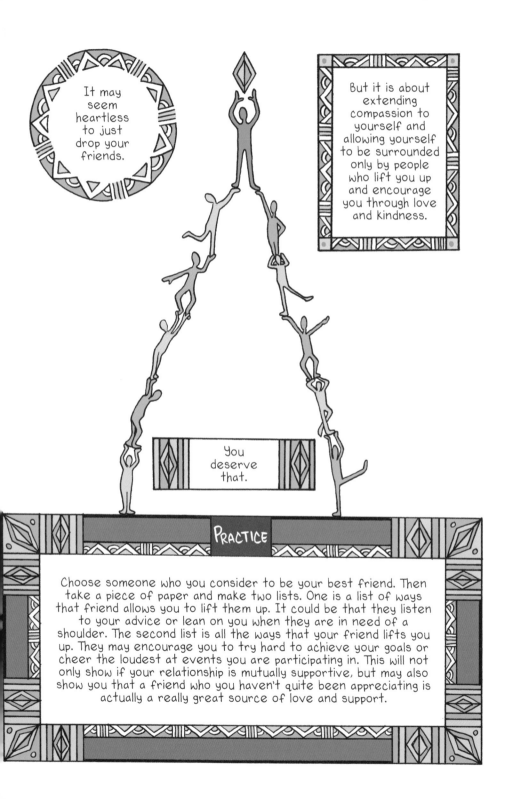

It may seem heartless to just drop your friends.

But it is about extending compassion to yourself and allowing yourself to be surrounded only by people who lift you up and encourage you through love and kindness.

You deserve that.

PRACTICE

Choose someone who you consider to be your best friend. Then take a piece of paper and make two lists. One is a list of ways that friend allows you to lift them up. It could be that they listen to your advice or lean on you when they are in need of a shoulder. The second list is all the ways that your friend lifts you up. They may encourage you to try hard to achieve your goals or cheer the loudest at events you are participating in. This will not only show if your relationship is mutually supportive, but may also show you that a friend who you haven't quite been appreciating is actually a really great source of love and support.

TECHNOLOGY is a part of our lives in an undeniable way.

As technology evolves, some people use it to help them in almost every facet of their lives.

It is not uncommon for people to spend nearly fifty percent of their day staring at a screen.

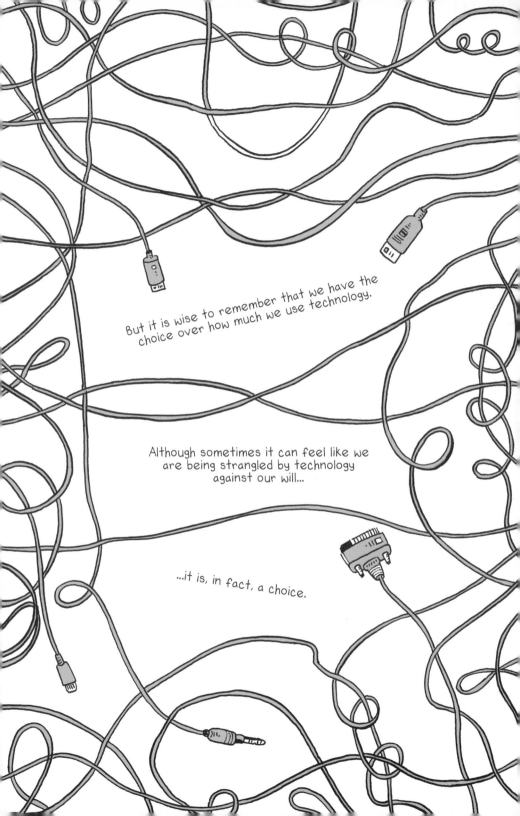

But it is wise to remember that we have the choice over how much we use technology.

Although sometimes it can feel like we are being strangled by technology against our will...

...it is, in fact, a choice.

But don't let this upset you. You are in control.

Don't miss out on real tangible life.

But don't assume that all technology is inherently bad.

Find a balance that allows you to utilise the benefits of technology while still being present in this endlessly beautiful world.

Balance is the key.

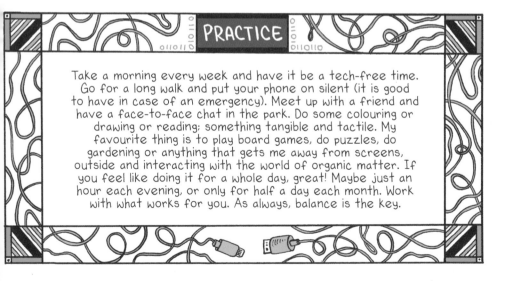

PRACTICE

Take a morning every week and have it be a tech-free time. Go for a long walk and put your phone on silent (it is good to have in case of an emergency). Meet up with a friend and have a face-to-face chat in the park. Do some colouring or drawing or reading; something tangible and tactile. My favourite thing is to play board games, do puzzles, do gardening or anything that gets me away from screens, outside and interacting with the world of organic matter. If you feel like doing it for a whole day, great! Maybe just an hour each evening, or only for half a day each month. Work with what works for you. As always, balance is the key.

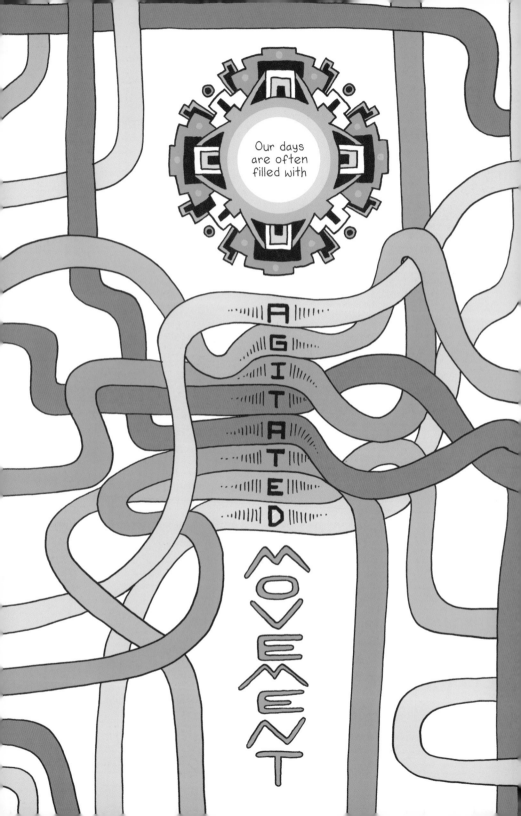

Our days
are often
filled with

AGITATED

MOVEMENT

In Zen Buddhism, meditation is referred to as "sitting just to sit". Not to achieve anything. But just to sit. Just to be.

The idea is that we have removed all agitated movement and we are simply left sitting.

And when we have stillness in our bodies, our mind has a chance to become still as well.

This is our entry point to our inner self.

When the outside world is still, we get a clear view into ourselves.

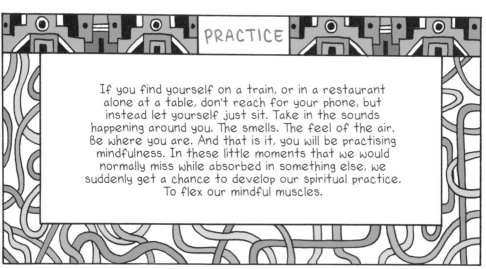

PRACTICE

If you find yourself on a train, or in a restaurant alone at a table, don't reach for your phone, but instead let yourself just sit. Take in the sounds happening around you. The smells. The feel of the air. Be where you are. And that is it, you will be practising mindfulness. In these little moments that we would normally miss while absorbed in something else, we suddenly get a chance to develop our spiritual practice. To flex our mindful muscles.

SIMPLICITY

is wonderfully sustainable.

Instead of adding things to your life that will keep you busy and run you off your feet, try taking things away.

TO DO LIST:

Instead of constantly adding opinions to your brain, try minimising your opinions and just being open to the experience of life.

Simplify.

Simplify.

Simplify.

And life will start to become much simpler.

In this simplicity, we will find ourselves being more present, not always worrying about the million things we have to do or acquire or achieve.

Mindfulness brings this simplicity out.

It shows us that the recipe for happiness and contentment is as simple as being present, focusing on our breathing and concentrating on the moment we are in.

So simple.

Do not fear that if you simplify, you are not making the most of your life.

Not achieving enough.

That you are lazy or squandering your potential.

That if you are not broken and tired and wound up in mental knots at the end of your day, you are not doing it right.

There is no achievement that surpasses a single moment of mindfulness.

There is no success like being present with a clear mind and heart.

And from this place of simplicity, you will start acting naturally, uncovering your very nature.

When you don't force your actions, they will begin to feel natural.

When simplicity is the aim, there is very little that cannot be achieved.

PRACTICE

In your head, picture what a perfect relaxing day for you would look like. Would you have time to have a long breakfast and read the paper? Or spend hours on the beach with your friends, going between swimming in the ocean and lying in the sun? Envision a lounging day from morning till night, all the activities you would do. Then, moving forward, try to bring more of those activities into your day, every day, while at the same time cutting out any unnecessary activities that you do not find fulfilling or relaxing. Enjoying your life in a healthy, sustainable way is perfectly acceptable.

PART THREE

AUTUMN

As the leaves begin to change colour and drop to the earth, autumn reminds us of the cycles of a life. But also of all the beautiful colours that make up this world.

In part three, we will explore the following topics:

Anxiety
Compassion
One's Own Nature
Breathing
Suffering
The Ego

 **THE PAST**

 **THE FUTURE**

 **FEAR**

 **HOPE**

 **CHANGE**

 **LOSS**

 **SUFFERING**

   **STUFF**

When we look back on the events of our past and are sad or embarrassed at how they happened.

Or when we look to the unknown future and try to predict how it will play out.

Sure that if our life goes one way we will definitely be happy or if it goes another all our chances of happiness will disappear.

Instead, we must learn to live our lives within uncertainty.

And learn to love watching things unfold without grasping or trying to control them.

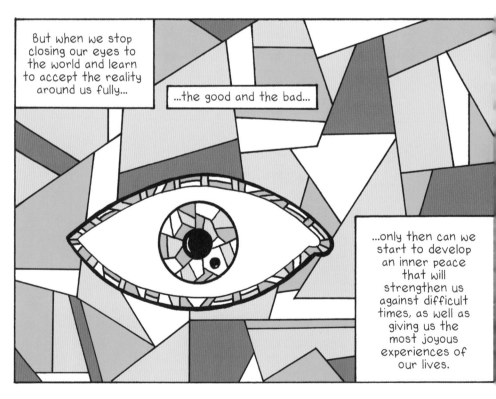

There is only ever the reality around us. If we can learn to accept the way things are and work with whatever arises, then events lose their ability to change our state of mind.

To cause us anxiety.

Learning to react to reality with openness and acceptance will keep anxiety at bay, and even turns the ever-changing world of circumstances into a game that tests our ability to move with the flow of things instead of constantly feeling like life is working against us.

PRACTICE

As anxieties arise, try to label them. If you get mud on the carpet, instead of fearing that you have ruined your whole house and therefore your whole life forever, look at the mud and label the anxiety that arises as a desire to keep things perfect in a world that is always moving between clean and dirty. Perfect and imperfect. I like to think of events as a broken dish. In the past, when a dish slipped out of my hand and broke, I would get upset with myself. Why am I so clumsy? But the reality is that when a plate breaks, it is broken and can never go back to being fully unbroken. That is an undeniable fact. I label that as a lesson in impermanence and a chance to practise letting things go. In this life, things are always breaking and ending, and at the same time things are always forming and beginning.

COMPASSION is at the heart of how to live a balanced and loving life.

It is the pursuit, above all others, that should inform every action of every moment of our day.

It should inform what we do with our time,

what we eat,

buy

or wear.

The most important thing about compassion is how we use it while interacting with all other beings.

Not just humans, but every lifeform that we come into contact with.

In order to extend compassion outwards, we first need to have compassion for ourselves. This is not just letting ourselves off the hook for things we may have done that caused suffering. Instead, we need to really acknowledge our hurtful actions. Look at them directly and say:

I did these things and they caused damage.

But it is not the end of the world. Flawed actions are a defining characteristic of being human.

Today I will do better.

Today I will act with compassion.

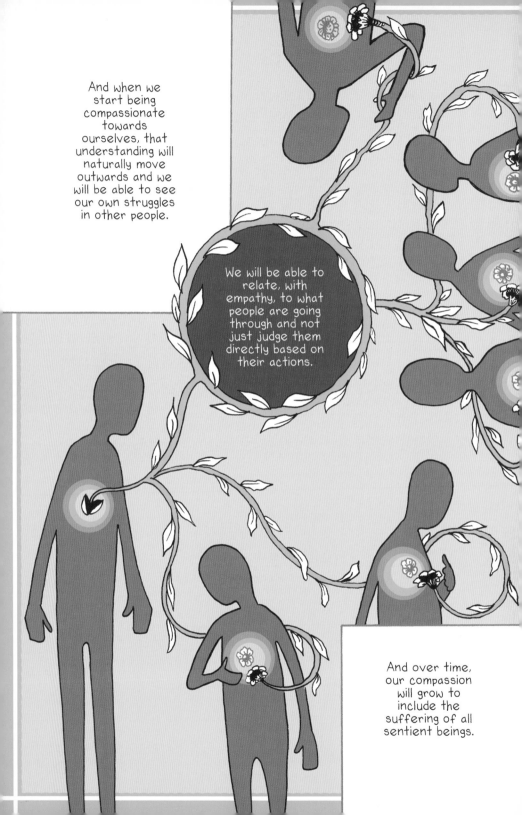

And when we start being compassionate towards ourselves, that understanding will naturally move outwards and we will be able to see our own struggles in other people.

We will be able to relate, with empathy, to what people are going through and not just judge them directly based on their actions.

And over time, our compassion will grow to include the suffering of all sentient beings.

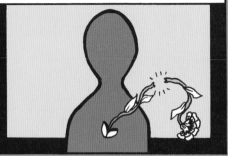

If we cut off our compassion in any way, then it will not have a chance to fully blossom.

And we will instead sink slowly into our own internal suffering.

Using compassion to ease the suffering of ourselves and others keeps us afloat and balanced.

And through that we become a vessel for love.

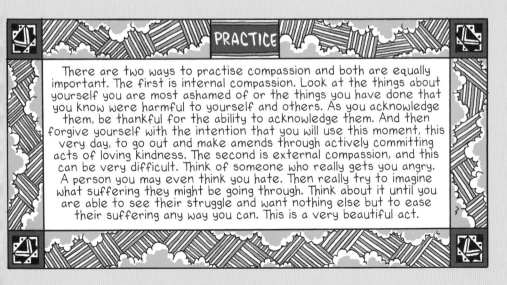

PRACTICE

There are two ways to practise compassion and both are equally important. The first is internal compassion. Look at the things about yourself you are most ashamed of or the things you have done that you know were harmful to yourself and others. As you acknowledge them, be thankful for the ability to acknowledge them. And then forgive yourself with the intention that you will use this moment, this very day, to go out and make amends through actively committing acts of loving kindness. The second is external compassion, and this can be very difficult. Think of someone who really gets you angry. A person you may even think you hate. Then really try to imagine what suffering they might be going through. Think about it until you are able to see their struggle and want nothing else but to ease their suffering any way you can. This is a very beautiful act.

ONE'S OWN

NATURE

already exists within one's self.

At the core of each of our beings is our

NATURE.

And uncovering it is a lifetime's work.

But a work that results in being fully alive. Being fully ourselves.

In the most natural of ways.

Many people's nature may be to look at the world scientifically. But each person will have a different perspective on scientific thinking.

Some people may approach science with a deep curiosity to discover new things.

While other people may approach science with a hope to ease suffering.

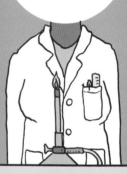

Then within that:

One person may intend to help people by finding cures for their illnesses.

While another wants to use science to protect and heal the earth.

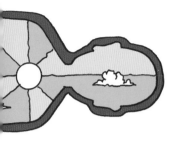

There are so many variations to everything, and no two people have the same nature.

In Taoist teachings, it is said that in order to discover one's nature one must act naturally.

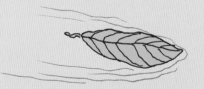

But how do we go about acting naturally?

To discover our natural self, we must act from that most indefinable of places: one's heart. And the way to act from the heart is to act with intuition.

Through easing our control over our actions and letting our mind, body and spirit act spontaneously...

...we begin to see our nature come through.

We all already know how to turn from a seed into a seedling into a blossoming beautiful flower.

  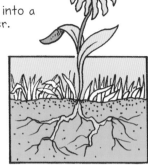

We just need to practise getting out of our own way and letting our nature come through.

And when it does, it will feel like the most natural thing in the world.

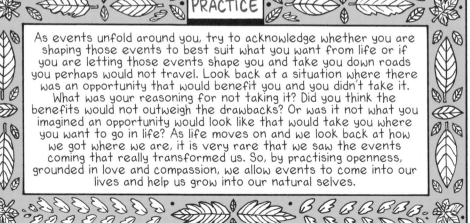

PRACTICE

As events unfold around you, try to acknowledge whether you are shaping those events to best suit what you want from life or if you are letting those events shape you and take you down roads you perhaps would not travel. Look back at a situation where there was an opportunity that would benefit you and you didn't take it. What was your reasoning for not taking it? Did you think the benefits would not outweigh the drawbacks? Or was it not what you imagined an opportunity would look like that would take you where you want to go in life? As life moves on and we look back at how we got where we are, it is very rare that we saw the events coming that really transformed us. So, by practising openness, grounded in love and compassion, we allow events to come into our lives and help us grow into our natural selves.

BREATHING

is a tool to help with mindfulness that we always have with us.

Something we can use to instantly connect with the present moment.

When our minds are racing and our thoughts are swirling and we seem to be as far away from the present moment as one can possibly get, we just need to come back to our breath.

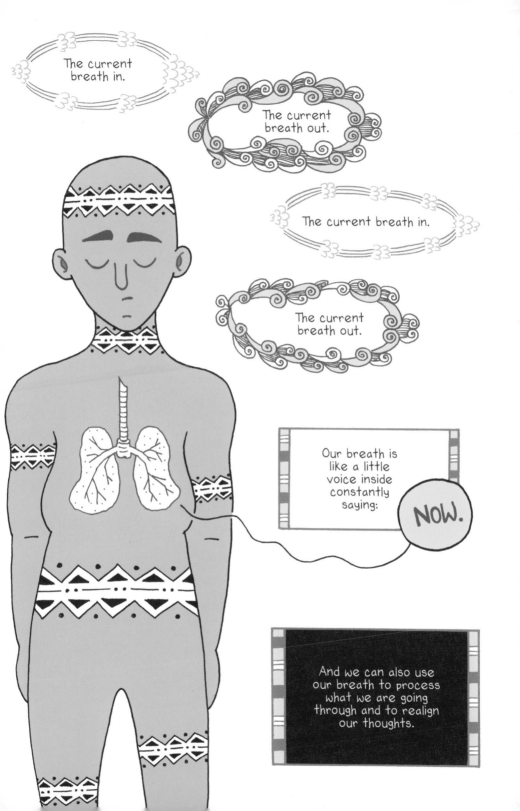

If you are anxious or upset about something in your life or that is happening in the world, you can breathe in. As you breathe in, acknowledge that you are taking in all your fear and anxiety. Do not push it away, but instead welcome it in fully. If we can't fully acknowledge our suffering or anxiety, then we can never move past it.

Then, as you breathe out, picture that you have filtered those negative emotions through your body and are now breathing out feelings of loving kindness and calm. Feelings that are not just to make you feel better, but to be offered out to the whole world.

In this way, each breath in filters the world's trouble.

And each breath out fills the world with emotional strength and love.

PRACTICE

Find a comfortable and quiet place to sit. Close your eyes. Focus and relax each part of your body from the head down. Once you are fully relaxed, turn your focus to your breath. Breathe in through your nose slowly, steadily and deeply. Then breathe out through your mouth, having your mouth open no more than would be necessary to slip a penny in. Breathe in for the count of five. Breathe out for the count of five. After you do this a few times, start breathing in and out as you count to six. Then seven. Then eight. This will help you develop your ability to concentrate on your breath and allow you to bring yourself into a deeper state of relaxation. Then later, as you are out in the busy world, you will be able to tap into that relaxation by simply stopping and breathing.

SUFFERING

is as much a part of life as breathing.

But we can stop suffering and won't suffocate.

SIGH!

When we ease the grip that suffering has on our lives, it is as if we take a deep breath. A sigh of relief.

And just be.

Just breathe.

But avoiding suffering only serves to strengthen its hold on our lives.

The more we ignore it, the more opportunity the suffering has to take greater hold of our hearts and minds.

Before long, the shadow of

SUFFERING

clouds all our thoughts and rains down on all our experiences.

Practising mindfulness allows us time to sit and breathe.

To breathe into our suffering. To really experience it, instead of running away from it.

To let it into our hearts with open arms.

This softness is the antidote to suffering.

Let it in.

Feel it fully.

Cry.

Weep.

Scream.

Give suffering a place to rest its head and before long we see that suffering is merely a manifestation of our own minds. It comes out of our being and so its home will always be within us.

PRACTICE

As you are going about your life and feel something arise within you that you may want to avoid, stop and let the feelings wash over you. Look at them directly. Live within them, as they are living within you. And as you breathe through the feelings, give them space to float around within you and you will find that they don't seem as scary as they appeared. Before long, they will even take on a lightness and as you mindfully observe them you will find that you are present, and in being present you are alive in the only thing that ever really exists: the moment you are in. Then get on with your day.

MOVING AWAY FROM THE **EGO**

is the biggest bridge we have to cross before we can live a consistently mindful life.

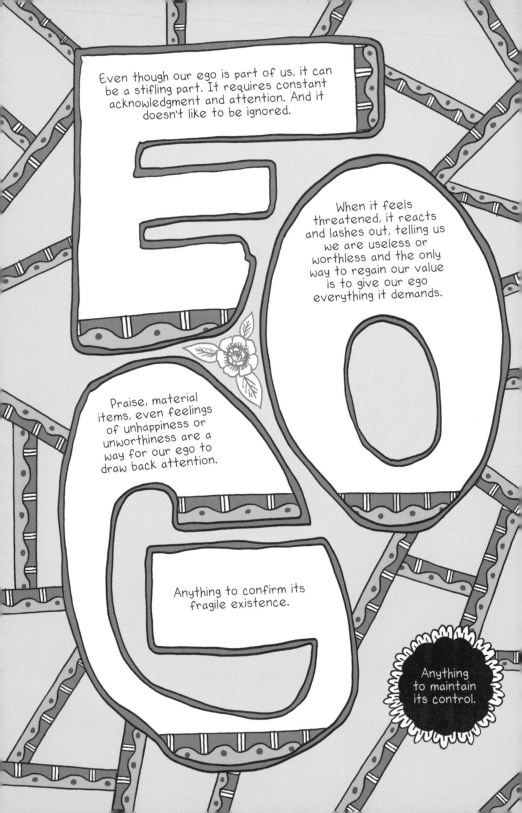

Even though our ego is part of us, it can be a stifling part. It requires constant acknowledgment and attention. And it doesn't like to be ignored.

When it feels threatened, it reacts and lashes out, telling us we are useless or worthless and the only way to regain our value is to give our ego everything it demands.

Praise, material items, even feelings of unhappiness or unworthiness are a way for our ego to draw back attention.

Anything to confirm its fragile existence.

Anything to maintain its control.

But when we spend less time focusing on

OUR

EGO

and more time focusing on

THE

MOMENT

we are living in,

we find that there is no need to define ourselves so strictly. No need to be imprisoned by our individual identity.

Instead, we can just exist. Just breathe. Just be.

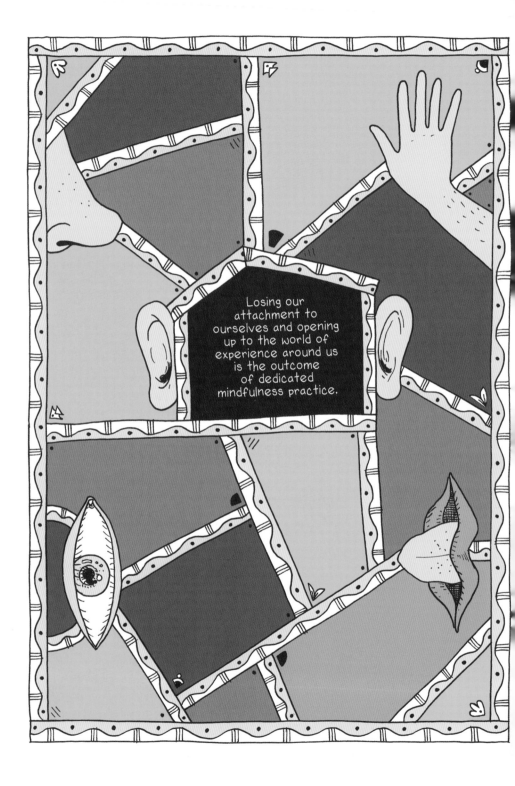

This is not to say that who you are as an individual is unimportant. But more that we spend so much of our time defining and indulging our ego that we miss the experience of life.

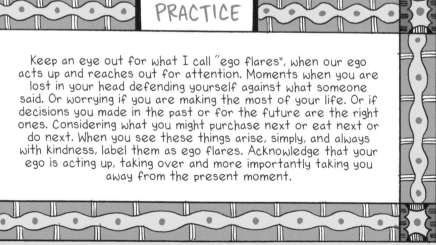

PRACTICE

Keep an eye out for what I call "ego flares", when our ego acts up and reaches out for attention. Moments when you are lost in your head defending yourself against what someone said. Or worrying if you are making the most of your life. Or if decisions you made in the past or for the future are the right ones. Considering what you might purchase next or eat next or do next. When you see these things arise, simply, and always with kindness, label them as ego flares. Acknowledge that your ego is acting up, taking over and more importantly taking you away from the present moment.

PART FOUR

WINTER

Winter is a time to rest, to turn inwards and reflect upon the changes that come throughout a year.

In part four, we will explore the following topics:

Nature
Humility
Lessons in Everything
Anger
Impermanence
Inner Peace

NATURE

is not
an escape.

It is a
return.

A coming
home.

So many of the problems we face in ourselves
and in the world today are the result of our
disconnection from the natural world.

In modern life, we look at nature as something outside of us, and very often feel more comfortable surrounded by human-made objects.

Those luxuries are comforting, but nothing can replace the touch of soil on our hands and feet.

The rain on our skin.

The wind blowing through our hair.

The sun.

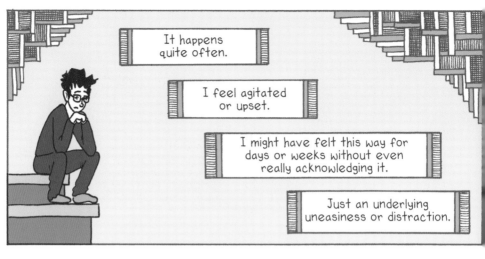

It happens quite often.

I feel agitated or upset.

I might have felt this way for days or weeks without even really acknowledging it.

Just an underlying uneasiness or distraction.

Then, all of a sudden, I might be out on a walk or in a garden.

I might see a bird fly overhead...

...or pick up a pile of soil in my hand, and the anxiety just melts away.

Like a thin layer of ice dissolved by the sun.

I realise that this is it.

To be alive is to experience the rhythms of nature.

I am often struck with a deep understanding that my ambition, fear, hope, dreams all serve to distract me from the very simple act of being present in nature and simply watching it all play out.

THIS LIFE COMES AND IT GOES.

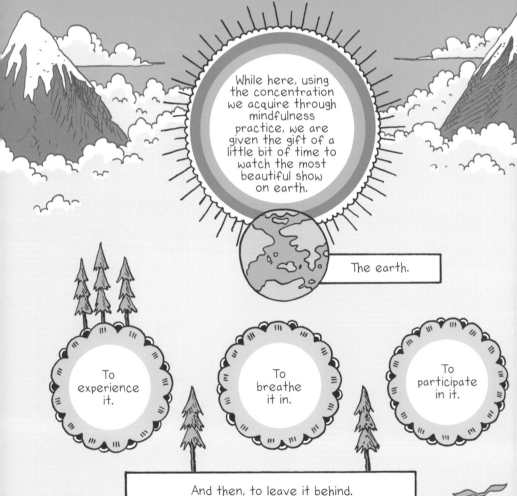

While here, using the concentration we acquire through mindfulness practice, we are given the gift of a little bit of time to watch the most beautiful show on earth.

The earth.

To experience it.

To breathe it in.

To participate in it.

And then, to leave it behind.

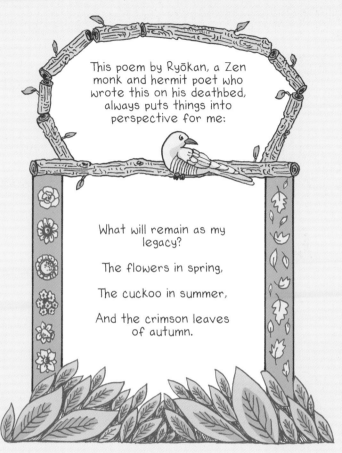

This poem by Ryōkan, a Zen monk and hermit poet who wrote this on his deathbed, always puts things into perspective for me:

What will remain as my legacy?

The flowers in spring,

The cuckoo in summer,

And the crimson leaves of autumn.

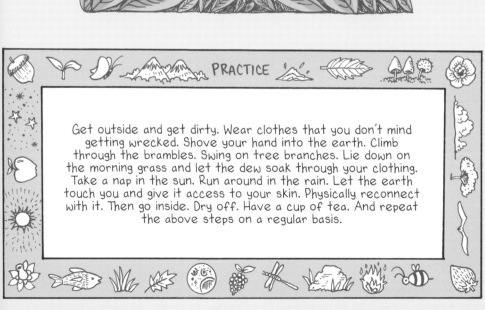

PRACTICE

Get outside and get dirty. Wear clothes that you don't mind getting wrecked. Shove your hand into the earth. Climb through the brambles. Swing on tree branches. Lie down on the morning grass and let the dew soak through your clothing. Take a nap in the sun. Run around in the rain. Let the earth touch you and give it access to your skin. Physically reconnect with it. Then go inside. Dry off. Have a cup of tea. And repeat the above steps on a regular basis.

HUMILITY

may appear to be a weakness,

but it is actually a strength that can open our hearts.

Knowing how to accept that we are not perfect, that we make mistakes and get things wrong, will allow us to grow in a way that is both nurturing and constructive to our being.

You will never meet a human being who is perfect. But every human being you meet is human. And therefore prone to error. Through humility, we can let the fact that we are human not hold us back from the positive change we can make in this world.

PRACTICE

If there is something you do or think that causes you to feel embarrassed, laugh out loud about it. In that laughter, try to really feel the lightness of it and the fact that it is a part of who you are as a whole. At the same time, if there is something you do or think that causes pain or negativity, then challenge those actions. With the same gentleness and humour, forgive yourself while also creating an intention in your mind to let go of the things you do that are harmful. And, at the end of it all, simply be grateful for a chance to be alive and to experience your faults. To be alive and have the chance to work on who you are, and how much laughter and light you can create with your life.

THERE ARE LITERALLY

LESSONS

IN

EVERYTHING

Wisdom shows us that no experience is a complete waste of time.

A total disaster.

Something to leave behind and forget about.

If we learn to see a lesson in everything, then even a seemingly trivial event can help us to make the most of our lives.

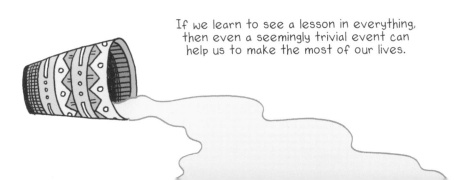

In a practical way, I try to keep at least one of the skills I acquire from every job I have.

Working in a clothing store taught me how to meticulously fold my laundry.

Working at a grocery store taught me to look at the back for the freshest products.

Cheeky, I know!

BREAD

Working at a coffee shop taught me how to multitask.

Working at a comic book shop taught me how to keep my finances in order.

TOTAL:

Working as a landscaper taught me how to tend a garden.

Working in publishing taught me what publishers are looking for when commissioning books.

MARKETING STRATEGY

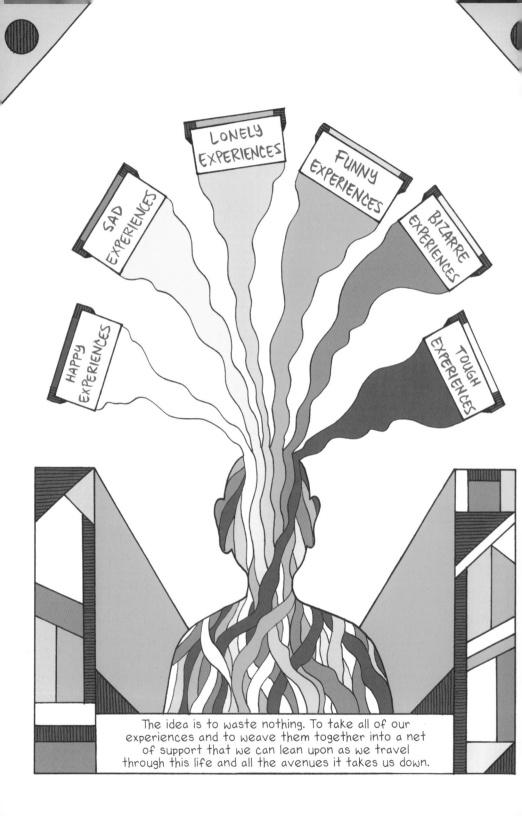

The idea is to waste nothing. To take all of our experiences and to weave them together into a net of support that we can lean upon as we travel through this life and all the avenues it takes us down.

And there are also spiritual lessons around us all of the time.

To me, the most poignant is the morning dew.

Each morning, the grass is covered in a delicate layer of dew.

But as the sun rises and life stirs, the dew disappears, leaving little to no trace of its existence.

This daily coming and going of the dew is a wonderful lesson in the ephemeral nature of life. We come into this world, get to glimpse the bright light of our existence and then pass by like a cloud in the sky.

The lesson is to be here while we are.

PRACTICE

Take a piece of paper or a notebook and write down all the lessons you have learned in this life and where you learned them from. Lessons learnt at school, at a job, from nature or from a friend or loved one. Be it how your grandma taught you to make baked pasta. Or how your father showed you how to fertilise flowers. How the rain taught you to appreciate your comfortable house. Or how your dog showed you how to be content with very little. Not only will this help to keep track of the lessons this life has provided you, but it will also keep track of precious moments when you interacted with the world and were given the gift of experience and knowledge.

ANGER

is a fruitless emotion.

It arises like a great fire, but when it leaves we are only sore and burned and the world around us is either a little more miserable or barely takes any notice.

If we feel anger towards other people, we hope that that anger will hurt them instead of ourselves, that a fire within ourselves will somehow burn the person we are angry towards more than it burns us.

It never does.

PEMA Chödrön

(an inspirational writer and spiritual leader)

describes anger perfectly.

She says that when we are angry towards another person, it is like picking up a hot coal with our bare hands.

And throwing it at them.

It may hit them and burn them.

It may miss them completely.

But we are guaranteed to get burned.

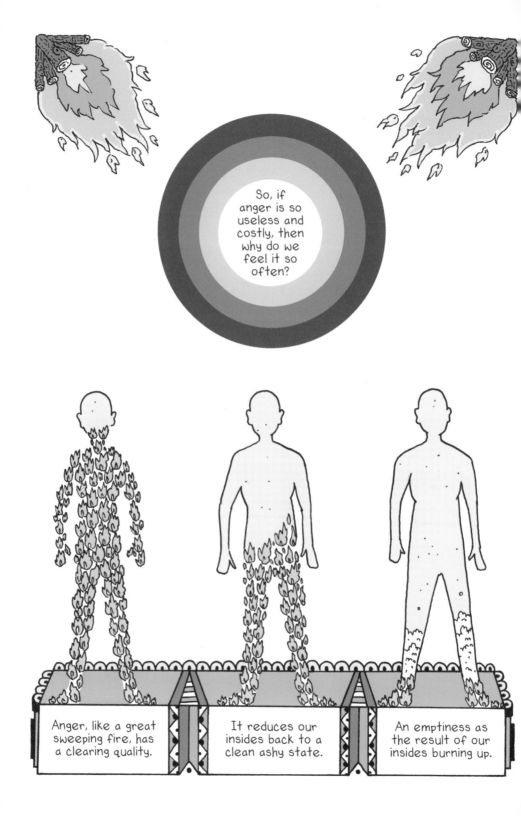

This emptiness is a place where we can start again.

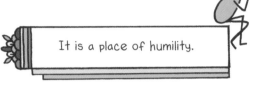

It is a place of humility.

An inevitable reminder that we are human and fallible.

And from there, we can start again towards filling ourselves with more constructive qualities like love and compassion.

But it is unwise to indulge that anger, for it burns up everything we have inside. It doesn't just clear us of fury and hate, but also of the good and kind qualities we have manifested.

IF **ANGER** comes, acknowledge it. Bow to it.

Then pick yourself up.

Dust off the ash.

And start climbing the hill of your heart back to your more loving self.

PRACTICE

Take some time when you are feeling happy and try to get angry. Sit and think of all the people who you believe have wronged you or irritated you. All the injustices you have experienced or read about. All the terrible acts of violence, war and oppression that occur in this world as the result of people's greed or desire. Try to turn your mind from happiness to hatred. It will feel awful. There may even be a sick feeling in your stomach that says, "No! I am happy, why would I want to be angry unnecessarily?" Then hold on to that feeling and the next time you are faced with a situation that might anger you, try to bring up that thought. Try to ask yourself: Do I want to feel anger right now? Or would I rather feel love despite this situation? It is a tough task, but well worth the effort.

IMPERMANENCE

is the main reason for mindfulness.

So we miss as few moments as possible of our limited lifetime.

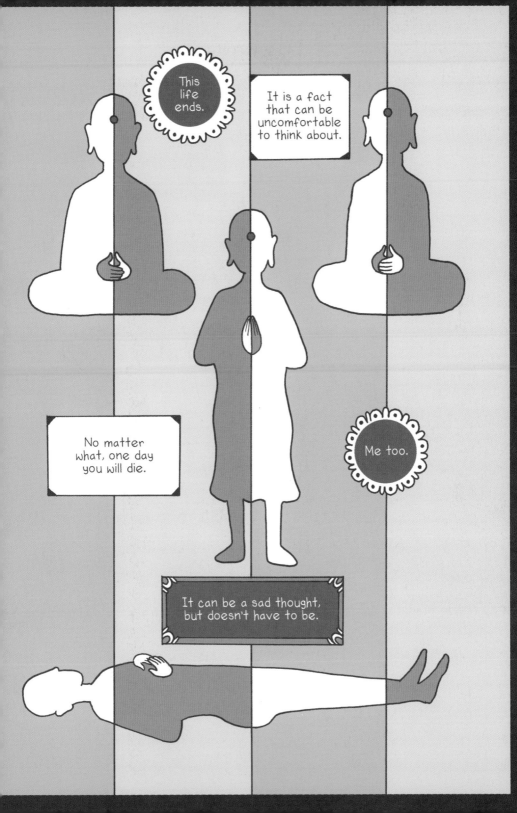

I remind myself that I am going to die every single day.

Often several times a day.

It is a way to remind myself that I am alive. That this is happening.

Right now.

It makes me stop, breathe, look around and be awed, on a daily basis, that I get to experience this world.

All its wonder.

Horror.

Magic.

And love.

What a gift.

But a gift I cannot hold on to.

If you are scared or sad to no longer be alive,
consider how things were before you were born.

Did you
suffer?

Or were
you at
peace?

I find this a comforting thought.

In a way, this life
is a break in the
status quo, and
when it is over we
simply return
to where we
came from.

Impermanence need not only apply to life and death.

Each day, there are little things that end.

Each moment, once it has passed, is gone forever.

Little deaths along the way.

If we can become comfortable with the ever-changing nature of the world, then peace will always exist in our hearts despite external circumstances.

Learning to let go of things with grace...

...allows us not to cling desperately to existence, but instead to be at ease in the passing of time.

The changing of the seasons.

The impermanence of ourselves and all beings.

PRACTICE

As you are going about your life and come upon a situation when things are ending, make a point to acknowledge it. If you are getting on a plane after a vacation, tell yourself, "I will never return to this place in these exact circumstances." Or if you are having your last ever class in a semester, tell yourself, "I will never be in this class again." Or on each birthday, you can tell yourself, "This is the last time I will turn this age." If we learn to be comfortable with things ending, then we will be able to remember that leaving this life will be just another ending.

INNER PEACE

is untouchable, once acquired.

It may get clouded over by the ebbs and flows of our thoughts and emotions, but it is a place inside ourselves that remains whole and happy despite what the outside world throws at us.

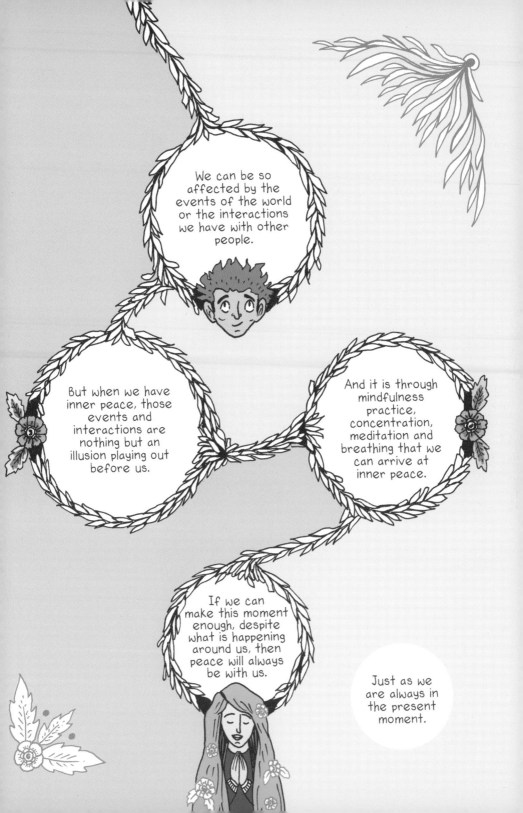

A key to inner peace is to take time to journey within.

To face our demons.

Shine our inner light and stop competing with the outside world.

I often remind myself of this quote from the Tao Te Ching:

If you compete with no one, no one can compete with you.

Walk your own path.

Be confident in yourself.

Use inner strength to lift you up when the world tries to knock you down.

When we have peace in our hearts...

...there is nowhere that is not home.

PRACTICE

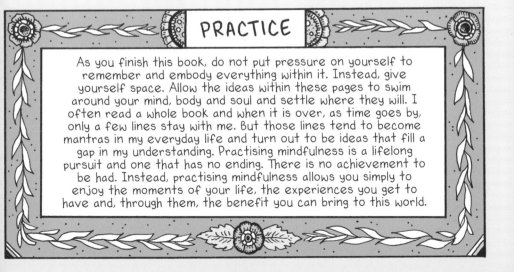

As you finish this book, do not put pressure on yourself to remember and embody everything within it. Instead, give yourself space. Allow the ideas within these pages to swim around your mind, body and soul and settle where they will. I often read a whole book and when it is over, as time goes by, only a few lines stay with me. But those lines tend to become mantras in my everyday life and turn out to be ideas that fill a gap in my understanding. Practising mindfulness is a lifelong pursuit and one that has no ending. There is no achievement to be had. Instead, practising mindfulness allows you simply to enjoy the moments of your life, the experiences you get to have and, through them, the benefit you can bring to this world.

But, of course,
the snows of winter
melt, moistening the
earth in preparation for
the buds of spring.

Mike Medaglia is an artist and Zen Buddhist practitioner, and the author of the bestselling *One Year Wiser* series. He has drawn comics on the theme of mindfulness for *The Huffington Post* and *The Elephant Journal*, among others, and hosts regular creative workshops. He posts regular illustrated meditations at oneyearwiser.com.

Photo by Elou Carroll

ALSO AVAILABLE IN THE SERIES

*365 Illustrated
Meditations*
ISBN 978-1-910593-01-1
368pp, Hardback

The Colouring Book
ISBN 978-1-910593-07-3
US Edition
ISBN 978-1-910593-14-1
112pp, Paperback

A Gratitude Journal
ISBN 978-1-910593-21-9
240pp, Hardback

oneyearwiser.com

ONE
YEAR
WISER